THE ENTREPRENEUR'S GUIDE TO *Having a Boss*

The ultimate roadmap for ambitious professionals.

DR. KYLE FIELDS

Contents

Chapter 1: Introduction

Chapter 2: The Benefits of Having a Boss

Chapter 3: Building a Relationship with Your Boss

Chapter 4: Dealing with a Difficult Boss

Chapter 5: Leveraging Your Boss's Experience

Chapter 6: When It's Time to Move On

Chapter 7: Always Have a Lateral Move

Chapter 8: Making the Most of Your Transition

Chapter 9: Thriving as an Entrepreneur

CHAPTER ONE:

INTRODUCTION

> "The journey of a thousand miles begins with one step."
>
> – Lao Tzu

In a world obsessed with the hustle of entrepreneurship, we often forget that not everyone is meant to be a founder or CEO, at least not right away. The truth is, success isn't limited to those who start their own businesses. Working for someone else can offer the stability, experience, and resources needed to fuel your entrepreneurial journey.

"The Entrepreneur's Guide to Having a Boss" flips the script on the idea that you have to go solo to succeed. Corporate jobs can teach invaluable skills—like managing teams, navigating office politics, and solving problems—that are key to running your own business later. In fact, working for a boss provides financial stability, networking opportunities, and mentorship that can fast-track your entrepreneurial growth.

As we explore this alternative path to entrepreneurship, we'll show you how to leverage your job for personal growth, learning, and business-building. You'll gain insights into developing a strong work ethic, handling office dynamics, and turning your boss into an asset. We'll also tackle how to run your position like a business as well as handling the emotional side of balancing your job with your entrepreneurial dreams and maintaining the motivation to pursue your goals.

[TWO]

This book isn't just about climbing the corporate ladder—it's about using your current role to build the foundation for future success. Whether you're just starting out or looking for fresh strategies to move forward, we'll guide you in making the most of your entrepreneurial journey, with a boss by your side.

[THREE]

CHAPTER TWO:

BENEFITS OF HAVING A BOSS

> "A Boss has the title, a leader has the people."
>
> — Simon Sinek

[FOUR]

Entrepreneurs often romanticize the idea of being their own boss, but the advantages of having a boss can be significant in achieving entrepreneurial goals. Having a boss can save time and money by allowing entrepreneurs to learn from their mistakes, receive valuable feedback, and avoid common pitfalls. This access to experience can fast-track learning, help improve decision-making, and increase the chances of success.

Resources & Expertise

A key benefit of having a boss is the opportunity to leverage their experience, knowledge, and industry connections. Bosses often have valuable resources—office space, equipment, and technology—that entrepreneurs may not have access to. They also provide insights into product development and market needs, allowing entrepreneurs to create successful offerings faster.

Structure & Accountability

Having a boss provides a clear structure and deadlines, which can help entrepreneurs manage their time and stay focused. The accountability to a boss ensures that tasks are prioritized and completed on schedule, improving productivity and minimizing the risk of getting off track.

[FIVE]

Mentorship & Guidance

A boss who acts as a mentor offers invaluable guidance, helping entrepreneurs learn faster and avoid costly mistakes. Through training, networking opportunities, and hands-on experience, entrepreneurs can gain practical insights into business development, leadership, and communication skills.

Stability

Beyond financial stability, having a boss provides emotional support, job security, and work-life balance. The predictability of working for someone else allows entrepreneurs to focus on personal well-being, reducing the stress that comes with the unpredictable nature of entrepreneurship.

Networking

Networking is crucial for business growth, and having a boss can open doors to industry connections that might otherwise be difficult to reach. A boss's established network can help entrepreneurs build relationships with potential clients, customers, and partners, creating new business opportunities.

Professional Development

Working under a boss provides access to professional development opportunities, such as training, workshops, and industry events. This not only helps entrepreneurs enhance their current skills but also prepares them for future entrepreneurial endeavors by gaining broader industry knowledge

[SIX]

Work-Life Balance

Having a boss can contribute to better work-life balance by setting a clear schedule and delegating tasks. Entrepreneurs often struggle with work-life balance, but by working for someone else, they can establish boundaries, avoid burnout, and maintain personal time for themselves.

In summary, while the freedom of being your own boss is appealing, the support, guidance, and resources that come from having a boss can help entrepreneurs achieve success more efficiently and with greater stability.

[SEVEN]

CHAPTER THREE:

BUILDING A RELATIONSHIP WITH YOUR BOSS

> *"The most important thing in communication is hearing what isn't said."*
>
> *- Peter Drucker*

A positive relationship with your boss can be a powerful asset in the workplace. Whether you're an employee or an entrepreneur, building a good rapport with your boss can make work more enjoyable, provide opportunities for career advancement, and give you a reliable source of guidance. Navigating this relationship can be challenging, but with a thoughtful approach, you can foster a productive and supportive bond that contributes to your long-term success.

In this chapter, we'll explore how to build a strong, positive relationship with your boss through clear communication, respect, trust, initiative, and teamwork.

Communication is Paramount

Effective communication is the cornerstone of any professional relationship, especially with your boss. Establishing open, consistent communication allows for transparency, builds trust, and ensures you're aligned on goals and expectations.
- Keep Your Boss Informed
- Seek Feedback
- Address Issues Early
- Mind Your Body Language

[NINE]

Show Respect and Professionalism

Respect and professionalism are fundamental to building a successful working relationship with your boss. Your demeanor, reliability, and appearance contribute to the way you're perceived.

- <u>Be Punctual and Reliable:</u> Consistently arriving on time and meeting deadlines shows that you value your commitments and are dependable.

- <u>Dress Professionally:</u> Your appearance can influence how others perceive your level of professionalism.

- <u>Avoid Gossip and Negativity</u>: A professional demeanor means focusing on constructive conversations and solutions, rather than engaging in workplace gossip or negativity. By maintaining a positive outlook and treating colleagues with respect, you demonstrate maturity and reliability.

Build Trust

Trust is essential in any relationship, and it's especially critical in the workplace. Earning your boss's trust involves consistently demonstrating reliability, accountability, and honesty.

- Delivery on Your Promises
- Be Transparent

[TEN]

Take Initiative

Taking the initiative shows your boss that you're invested in the company's success and ready to contribute beyond your defined responsibilities.

- <u>Seek Out Opportunities:</u> Look for areas where you can add value, improve efficiency, or solve existing issues. Propose solutions, volunteer for projects, and take on responsibilities that demonstrate your commitment to growth and impact.

- <u>Communicate Your Ideas:</u> Share your ideas and plans with your boss and colleagues, promoting transparency and alignment. By presenting ideas clearly and welcoming feedback, you signal your readiness to contribute strategically.

- <u>Step Outside Your Comfort Zone:</u> Taking on new challenges may feel intimidating, but it's an essential part of growth. Show a willingness to take calculated risks and adapt to change, positioning yourself as a proactive leader within your team.

Demonstrating initiative not only boosts your visibility but also showcases your dedication to the organization's goals. This proactivity sets you apart and reinforces your value as an asset to the company.

[ELEVEN]

Be a Team Player

A successful working environment thrives on teamwork, and supporting your colleagues reflects well on you in your boss's eyes.

- Collaborate Actively: Engage with colleagues on joint projects and offer your assistance when appropriate. This shows that you're committed to the team's success, not just your individual achievements.

- Celebrate Team Wins: Recognize and appreciate the contributions of your teammates. Building positive relationships within the team contributes to a supportive workplace and demonstrates your investment in collective success.

- Maintain a Positive Attitude: Being solution-oriented, even in difficult situations, reflects resilience and maturity. Your boss will appreciate your role in fostering a collaborative, positive work environment.

By being a team player, you contribute to a workplace culture of support, collaboration, and shared success, enhancing your rapport with both your boss and your colleagues.

CHAPTER FOUR:

DEALING WITH A DIFFICULT BOSS

> *"Don't let the noise of others' opinions drown out your own inner voice."*
>
> *- Steve Jobs*

Dealing with a difficult boss is a challenge that many employees face at some point in their careers. While a good working relationship is ideal, not all bosses are easy to work with. However, with the right approach and strategies, it's possible to navigate these situations and even turn them into learning experiences.

A difficult boss can be a major source of stress, affecting your focus, performance, and overall well-being. Yet, not all difficult bosses are alike; some may simply be demanding or have a different management style than you're accustomed to, while others might create a toxic work environment. Regardless of the specific situation, approaching it with a calm, objective mindset is essential.

Identify the Problem

The first step in addressing a challenging relationship with your boss is to identify the core issue. Is your boss overly critical, unresponsive, or a micromanager? Understanding the specific behavior causing friction helps target the root of the problem instead of reacting to the symptoms alone.

Consider your boss's perspective as well. External pressures, personal issues, or high expectations from their own managers could be influencing their behavior. By seeing the full picture, you'll be better prepared to respond with empathy and find solutions that work for both of you.

[FOURTEEN]

Once you understand the problem, think about potential solutions. This could mean having a direct, respectful conversation with your boss, seeking advice from a mentor or HR, or finding ways to manage your own responses. Whatever route you take, maintaining professionalism is key.

Stay Calm

In high-pressure environments, remaining calm is crucial. When dealing with a difficult boss, it's essential to keep your emotions in check. Avoid letting frustration or anger cloud your reactions; instead, give yourself time to step back and reflect.

Focus on problem-solving rather than the emotional side of the conflict. Take breaks when needed, and remind yourself that staying composed will help you communicate more effectively. Avoid personal attacks, and focus on constructive feedback. If your boss's behavior crosses the line, stay calm but assertive as you communicate your boundaries.

Communicate Clearly

Clear communication is essential when working with a challenging boss. Outline your concerns specifically and provide examples when necessary. For instance, if your boss micromanages, you could highlight specific instances that have impacted productivity.

[FIFTEEN]

Offer practical solutions as well. Suggest areas where you can take more responsibility or adjustments that could improve workflow. Frame your concerns constructively, avoiding accusatory language. Actively listen to their feedback, which can build trust and improve collaboration.

Documenting conversations can be useful, especially if escalation becomes necessary. Written records of emails or meeting notes ensure clarity and consistency in follow-ups.

Set Boundaries

Setting boundaries is crucial for both productivity and well-being. To begin, identify behaviors that hinder your work, then decide on appropriate boundaries. Communicate these respectfully, explaining how the changes benefit your productivity and, ultimately, the team's success.

Use "I" statements rather than "you" statements to prevent defensiveness. For example, instead of "You're always interrupting me," try "I need uninterrupted time to focus on this project." Suggest compromises, such as weekly check-ins, to reduce interruptions while keeping your boss informed.

Remember that setting boundaries is an ongoing process. As your role and responsibilities evolve, you may need to adjust your boundaries accordingly.

[SIXTEEN]

Seek Support

Managing a difficult boss can be emotionally draining, so don't hesitate to seek support. Speaking with trusted colleagues, mentors, or friends can provide fresh perspectives and help you brainstorm solutions. Professional guidance, like therapy or counseling, can also help you manage stress and maintain resilience.

If the situation worsens or violates company policies, consider speaking to HR. They can offer guidance or intervene if necessary. Ultimately, if your work environment becomes intolerable, it may be time to explore other job opportunities.

[SEVENTEEN]

CHAPTER FIVE:

LEVERAGING YOUR BOSS'S EXPERIENCE

> "A mentor is someone who allows you to see the hope inside yourself."
>
> – Oprah Winfrey

[EIGHTTEEN]

When you're on an entrepreneurial journey, a supportive and experienced boss can be an invaluable asset. A boss who's invested in your growth offers guidance and insights that may be hard to find alone. They can help you avoid costly mistakes, refine your strategy, and serve as a sounding board through the ups and downs of starting a business.

But what defines a good boss in this context? Ideally, a good boss listens, provides constructive feedback, and has industry experience that allows them to offer actionable insights. They invest in your development and understand the nuances of entrepreneurship, guiding you as you navigate challenges and seize opportunities.

A supportive boss can also introduce you to their professional network, connecting you with mentors, investors, and potential clients or partners. These introductions can help you build relationships that drive your business forward, making your boss's experience a critical resource for professional growth.

Ask for Feedback

Seeking your boss's feedback is essential to refine your skills and enhance your performance. Approach feedback sessions with an open mind, ready to learn and improve, and don't hesitate to ask clarifying questions. The insights you gain can guide your professional development, helping you build a solid foundation for your entrepreneurial journey.

[NINETEEN]

Seek Advice

Your boss has likely faced many of the same challenges that you'll encounter. Don't hesitate to seek their advice, but come prepared with specific questions. Showing respect for their time and expertise, along with being attentive to their responses, demonstrates your commitment. Though your boss might not have all the answers, their insights can provide direction for your path forward.

Learn from Their Mistakes

Mistakes are inevitable, but learning from someone else's can save you from making the same ones. Approach your boss with a genuine interest in understanding what they've learned through trial and error. This proactive approach can help you avoid common pitfalls and establish a more resilient mindset, accepting mistakes as growth opportunities rather than setbacks.

Observe Their Leadership Style

Observing how your boss leads can provide a blueprint for your future role as a leader. Notice how they handle communication, conflict, delegation, and decision-making. If you have a good relationship, you can even ask them directly about their leadership philosophy. Understanding their style—whether authoritarian, democratic, laissez-faire, transformational, or situational—can inform your own leadership approach, helping you build a work environment that fosters success.

[TWENTY]

Network Through Their Connections

Networking is a cornerstone of entrepreneurship. Your boss likely has connections that can be valuable to your business. When you approach them, be clear about what you're seeking. Whether it's a potential client, an industry mentor, or a strategic partner, being specific about your goals shows respect for their time and can lead to meaningful introductions that expand your network and open doors for your business.

Building a Beneficial Relationship

Leveraging your boss's experience is not just about seeking guidance; it's about fostering a positive, mutually respectful relationship. Come prepared with thoughtful questions and show gratitude for their time and advice. This not only demonstrates your professionalism but also increases the likelihood that they'll continue to support your journey.

[TWENTY-ONE]

CHAPTER SIX:

WHEN IT'S TIME TO MOVE ON

> *"If you're not willing to risk the usual, you will have to settle for the ordinary.*
>
> *- Jim Rohn*

As an entrepreneur, knowing when to move on from your current job or boss is crucial for your growth and well-being. While leaving can be daunting, recognizing the signs that it's time to move on and handling your departure professionally can open doors to fulfilling opportunities.

Signs It May Be Time to Move On

- <u>Lack of Growth Opportunities:</u> If you feel stuck or stagnant with no new challenges, it's a clear sign that it may be time to seek new horizons. As an entrepreneur, continuous growth is essential. Reflect on whether you're acquiring the skills and experience you need to achieve your goals. If not, moving on may be the best option to keep advancing your career.

- <u>Misaligned Values:</u> Working in an environment where your values don't align with those of your company can drain your motivation. If you find yourself disagreeing with your company's direction or feeling unpassionate about the work, it's worth considering a transition to a job or business that aligns better with your beliefs. Assess whether reconciliation is possible or if leaving is necessary to maintain your integrity and drive.

[TWENTY-THREE]

Planning Your Transition

Leaving a job is a significant decision, so make it thoughtfully. Here are a few steps to ensure a smooth exit:

- Set Up a Plan: Whether you're starting your own business, joining another company, or pursuing additional education, having a clear plan is essential. Networking with industry professionals and reaching out to potential employers or clients is also helpful.

- Maintain Professionalism: When it's time to leave, provide ample notice—usually two weeks. Finish your responsibilities and complete outstanding projects to ensure a smooth transition. This leaves a positive impression and reflects well on your character.

- Preserve Relationships: Offer thanks for the experience, even if your journey had ups and downs. Maintaining positive connections is valuable, as your former colleagues may become future collaborators, clients, or advocates.

Embrace the Future

Leaving a job can be intimidating, but it also creates the space to pursue what you truly want. Trust your instincts, and be open to the new opportunities and challenges that lie ahead. With a thoughtful approach and positive mindset, moving on can be a pivotal step toward building a successful and fulfilling career.

[TWENTY-FOUR]

CHAPTER SEVEN:

ALWAYS HAVE A LATERAL MOVE

> "Knowledge is understanding it's a one-way street; Wisdom is looking both ways anyway."
>
> — Kyle Fields

[TWENTY-FIVE]

When we think about "lateral moves," it's typically within the context of advancing within an organization—a shift to a different department or role at the same level. However, a lateral move can be much broader than this. It can also mean having a backup or an alternative plan outside our current organization or job. This chapter delves into why having a lateral move—essentially a safety net—is crucial, how it can benefit our career, and the steps we can take to establish and maintain it.

The Need for a Lateral Move

A lateral move isn't just about preparing for a new job. It's about having a safety net—a readily accessible option outside of our current workplace that keeps us adaptable and resilient in an ever-evolving job market. In times of economic or organizational uncertainty, having a lateral move prepared can alleviate stress and provide peace of mind. With a backup option in place, we are more likely to feel secure and confident, which can empower us to take risks, pursue growth opportunities, and remain motivated.

Without options outside of our current role, we may feel "stuck" or stagnant, resulting in a lack of enthusiasm and decreased job satisfaction. A lateral move counteracts these feelings by providing alternative pathways. We're not limited to one role or one trajectory; instead, we're free to explore, stay engaged, and continuously broaden our skill set and perspective.

[TWENTY-SIX]

Having this safety net is also empowering. It prevents us from being solely dependent on one employer or supervisor. When we rely too heavily on a single position, we may find ourselves in situations where we feel unable to address conflicts or advocate for ourselves due to fear of jeopardizing our role. But with a lateral move ready, we can take greater control of our work environment.

The Benefits of a Lateral Move

When we prepare a lateral move, we're also building new skills, expanding our professional network, and developing a sense of autonomy. This move can offer:

- Job Security: We're less vulnerable to the dynamics of any single organization.

- Increased Agency: We maintain control over our career, reducing dependence on any one employer.

- Skill and Knowledge Growth: Lateral moves often introduce us to new fields or roles, adding depth and breadth to our abilities.

- Reduced Stress: Knowing we have options reduces career-related anxiety, freeing us to make decisions that align with our long-term goals.

- Networking Opportunities: Moving between roles and fields helps us forge diverse connections that may lead to unexpected career advancements or opportunities.

[TWENTY-SEVEN]

Creating and Maintaining a Lateral Move

So, how do we build and sustain this lateral move safety net?

- Expand Your Network: Actively engage in networking beyond your current role or industry. Attend conferences, join relevant online communities, and volunteer in areas that align with your interests. Networking is key, exposing you to new ideas and career paths you might not have considered. The broader and more diverse your network, the more opportunities are likely to come your way.

- Stay Updated on Skills: Industries evolve quickly, and to remain competitive, we need to keep our skills sharp and relevant. Consider courses, workshops, or certifications that align with both your current role and potential lateral moves. The more current your skills, the easier it will be to transition to new roles, especially in emerging fields.

- Remain Open to Change: Building a lateral move often requires stepping outside our comfort zone. We need to be ready to take risks, embrace challenges, and approach unfamiliar roles or industries. This flexibility not only opens doors to new opportunities but also strengthens our resilience and adaptability.

[TWENTY-EIGHT]

- Maintain an Open Mind: Keeping an open mind allows us to see opportunities where we might not expect them. It also encourages us to take calculated risks and venture into areas that may seem unfamiliar but could prove valuable. This openness is essential for creating a robust and adaptable career path.

Building a lateral move safety net is more than just a contingency plan; it's a strategic approach to career management. It empowers us to take control of our professional journey, positioning ourselves as valuable and flexible assets in any job market. By building a foundation that includes diverse skills, a solid network, and the willingness to step into new arenas, we gain the agency to navigate our careers with confidence and resilience.

Having a lateral move outside of our current job or organization ensures that we have options, security, and the freedom to make career decisions that serve us best. By actively seeking new opportunities, keeping our skills current, and maintaining flexibility, we create a career safety net that allows us to adapt to any challenge. Embracing this mindset enables us to lead our careers proactively, positioning us for success and fulfillment no matter what the future brings.

[TWENTY-NINE]

CHAPTER EIGHT:

MAKING THE MOST OF YOUR TRANSITION

> *"The secret of change is to focus all of your energy not on fighting the old but on building the new"*
>
> *- Socrates*

[THIRTY]

Leaving a job, especially after a long tenure or with a close-knit team, can feel overwhelming. Yet, it's also a prime opportunity for growth and reinvention as you embark on an entrepreneurial journey.

Reflect on Your Experience

Before diving into your new venture, take some time to reflect. Consider what you've learned, your successes, and even the challenges you've encountered. Think about the skills you honed and feedback you received from your boss and colleagues. Each lesson offers insights that can strengthen your approach as an entrepreneur. For instance, you might discover strategies that could benefit your business or identify areas for personal improvement.

Reflection isn't just about learning—it's also an exercise in gratitude. Acknowledging positive experiences helps you carry forward a sense of fulfillment and professionalism, which fuels a confident start in your new role.

Build and Strengthen Your Network

Transitioning into entrepreneurship doesn't mean leaving your old connections behind. In fact, your professional network is one of your greatest assets. Start by reaching out to former colleagues, supervisors, and industry contacts to let them know about your new endeavor. Stay connected through LinkedIn or regular emails, and consider attending both online and in-person networking events to meet new people in your industry.

These connections may lead to mentorship, collaboration, or even new clients. Building a strong network requires consistent effort, but it can play a crucial role in the growth and success of your business.

Stay in Touch and Show Appreciation

Leaving a job doesn't mean severing relationships. After your departure, send a thank-you note or email expressing appreciation for your time there. Offering your support for any future projects is a simple gesture that leaves a positive impression and keeps the door open for future collaborations.

Connecting on professional networks like LinkedIn allows you to celebrate each other's achievements and stay top of mind, which is valuable as your entrepreneurial journey progresses. A strong, ongoing relationship with former colleagues can be beneficial for referrals, potential partnerships, and future opportunities.

Set Clear Goals

During this transition, take time to set goals for your new entrepreneurial path. Define what you want to achieve and align your goals with the skills and insights you've gained from your previous role. SMART (Specific, Measurable, Achievable, Relevant, Time-bound) goals help keep you focused and motivated. Break down your objectives into actionable steps to track your progress and celebrate milestones along the way.

[THIRTY-TWO]

Embrace the Unknown

Starting fresh as an entrepreneur can stir up feelings of excitement and apprehension. Embrace this phase as a unique opportunity for growth. Take what you've learned from past experiences and apply it with an open mind. Don't be afraid to take calculated risks, experiment, and learn through trial and error. Remember, building a successful business is a journey that requires patience and persistence.

Celebrate your successes, no matter how small. Small wins add up and help keep your momentum going. When setbacks arise, view them as learning opportunities, and don't hesitate to seek guidance from mentors, peers, or advisors who can support you along the way.

Take Care of Yourself

Amidst the demands of transitioning and growing your business, self-care is essential. Make time for activities that recharge you— exercise, healthy meals, and relaxation. A healthy mind and body will enable you to tackle the challenges of entrepreneurship with resilience and focus.

Your transition is an exciting stepping stone toward realizing your entrepreneurial vision. Approach it with a positive mindset, connect with supportive people, and leverage your past experiences as valuable resources.

[THIRTY-THREE]

CHAPTER NINE:

THRIVING AS AN ENTREPENEUR

> "Happiness is the key to success.
> If you love what you are doing,
> you will be successful.
>
> - Albert Schweitzer

As an entrepreneur, leaving your previous job and boss behind can be both exhilarating and challenging. It's important to take some time to reflect on what you've learned, set new goals, and approach your new role with a positive attitude and confidence in your abilities.

One of the keys to thriving in your new role as an entrepreneur is to be proactive. Take the initiative to network, build relationships with potential clients and partners, and seek out new opportunities for growth. Don't be afraid to take risks and try new things, as this can lead to innovative ideas and breakthroughs.

It's also important to stay organized and focused on your priorities. Set clear goals and develop a plan for achieving them, and stay disciplined in your approach. This will help you stay on track and avoid distractions that can derail your progress. As you navigate your new role, remember to stay open to feedback and continue to learn and grow. Seek out mentors and advisors who can provide guidance and support, and be willing to adapt and evolve as your business evolves.

Finally, remember that success as an entrepreneur is often a journey, not a destination. Stay committed to your goals, stay positive and resilient in the face of challenges, and celebrate your successes along the way.

[THIRTY-FIVE]

Discover Your Niche

Finding your niche is a powerful way to stand out and succeed in a crowded market. By identifying your unique strengths, experiences, and skills, you can carve out a space that allows you to offer unparalleled value to your customers.

Reflect on what sets you apart from your competitors. What unique solutions can you provide that no one else does? Consider your background, personal experiences, and areas of expertise. Once you discover your niche, concentrate your efforts on building authority in that space—stay informed on industry trends, attend events, and connect with like-minded professionals. Over time, you'll build a reputation as a trusted expert in your field.

Keep in mind that niches can evolve. Stay flexible and open to opportunities as your business grows. The entrepreneurial landscape is dynamic, and by continually learning, you can ensure that your niche remains relevant.

Create a Business Plan

A well-crafted business plan is your entrepreneurial blueprint. It is much more than a task to tick off your to-do list—it's the foundation for your success. Crafting a detailed plan requires research, strategy, and a clear understanding of your market.

[THIRTY-SIX]

Begin with a compelling mission statement that defines your core values and vision. This should act as the cornerstone of your business. Next, conduct a market analysis to better understand your target audience and competitors. Define your marketing and sales strategies, financial projections, and the milestones you'll use to track progress. Regularly revisit and revise your plan to ensure it evolves with your business.

A solid business plan positions you for growth by giving you a clear path forward. It helps align your resources, set realistic goals, and identify the steps needed to reach them.

Build a Robust Team

Entrepreneurship doesn't have to be a solitary journey. Surrounding yourself with a strong team can provide invaluable support, expertise, and fresh perspectives. However, assembling the right team requires thoughtful planning.

When hiring, focus not only on skills but also on cultural fit. Seek individuals who share your vision and passion for your mission. A cohesive team that aligns with your company's values is more likely to work harmoniously and deliver exceptional results.

[THIRTY-SEVEN]

As a leader, your role is crucial. Provide clear direction, communicate openly, and create an environment of continuous learning and growth. A supportive team can greatly enhance your entrepreneurial success, but it's your leadership that ensures their collective success.

Embrace Failure

Entrepreneurship doesn't have to be a solitary journey. Surrounding yourself with a strong team can provide invaluable support, expertise, and fresh perspectives. However, assembling the right team requires thoughtful planning.

When hiring, focus not only on skills but also on cultural fit. Seek individuals who share your vision and passion for your mission. A cohesive team that aligns with your company's values is more likely to work harmoniously and deliver exceptional results.

As a leader, your role is crucial. Provide clear direction, communicate openly, and create an environment of continuous learning and growth. A supportive team can greatly enhance your entrepreneurial success, but it's your leadership that ensures their collective success.

Stay Focused

In the whirlwind of entrepreneurship, staying focused on your goals is essential. With so many tasks vying for your attention, it's easy to become distracted. To stay on track, prioritize your key objectives and develop a routine that supports them.

Organize your day around the most important tasks. Cultivate discipline to say "no" to opportunities or distractions that don't align with your core mission. By establishing systems for managing routine tasks—such as financial tracking, customer data, and inventory management—you free up time to focus on strategic decisions that move your business forward.

[THIRTY-NINE]

Network and Collaborate

Networking is more than just exchanging business cards—it's about building genuine, mutually beneficial relationships. Connecting with other entrepreneurs, industry professionals, and potential partners can open doors to new ideas, resources, and opportunities.

Attend events, join industry groups, and engage in online communities to expand your network. Collaboration can provide fresh insights and create synergies that accelerate growth. Seek opportunities to partner with others who complement your skills and vision, and don't be afraid to share knowledge and experiences.

Remember, the success of your business is often a team effort. By building a network of trusted allies and collaborators, you position yourself for greater success.

Conclusion

Building a successful business is a journey, not a destination. It is filled with triumphs and challenges, growth and setbacks, but with the right mindset and strategies, you can navigate the winding path of entrepreneurship and create something meaningful and sustainable. Throughout this book, we have explored the essential elements needed to thrive as an entrepreneur, from discovering your niche to building a robust team, embracing failure, and staying focused on your goals.

At the core of entrepreneurial success is resilience. No matter how many obstacles you encounter, it's crucial to stay adaptable, stay open to learning, and persist in the face of adversity. With each setback, there's an opportunity to learn, to pivot, and to refine your approach. This mindset is what will ultimately separate you from those who give up after the first hurdle.

As you move forward, remember that the foundation of your business starts with clarity—clarity in your mission, in your vision, and in the direction you want to take your company. A strong business plan will guide you, but flexibility will allow you to adapt to the changes in your market and environment. Your team will be your backbone, and your network will be your support system, each playing a vital role in your entrepreneurial success.

[FORTY-ONE]

The road to entrepreneurship is often lonely, but it doesn't have to be. Build relationships, network with other entrepreneurs, and seek mentorship. Collaboration is a powerful tool that can propel you forward, and finding the right people to surround yourself with can make all the difference.

Lastly, always remember that success doesn't come overnight. It's a marathon, not a sprint. Celebrate your wins, learn from your failures, and keep your eyes focused on your goals. With hard work, perseverance, and the right strategies in place, you can build the business of your dreams.

So, take a deep breath, trust your instincts, and step forward with confidence. The world of entrepreneurship is waiting for you. Now is your time to succeed.

[END]

All rights reserved. No part of this book may be reproduced, stored in a retrieval system, or transmitted in any form or by any means, electronic, mechanical, photocopying, recording, or otherwise, without the prior written permission of the publisher, except as provided by U.S. copyright law.

The information in this book is for educational purposes only. The author and publisher make no warranties or representations regarding the accuracy or completeness of the contents and assume no liability for any errors or omissions.

Printed in the United States of America
For more information or to contact the author, visit: KyleFields.com

Copyright © 2024 by Kyle Fields & Jacob Ross Publications, a Jacob Ross company.

Printed in Great Britain
by Amazon